UNIVERSE HAS GOT YOUR BACK

NEVER QUIT ! ABUNDANCE IS OUR BIRTH RIGHT

KINJAL PRAKASH PANCHOLI

DEDICATIED TO ENTIRE HUMANITY OF MOTHER GAIA WHO ARE READY TO AWAKEN AND UNITE AS ONE AND WHO DARE TO DREAM BIG AND ATTRACT UNLIMTED ABUNDANCE OF THE UNIVERSE BY BEING ONE WITH SOURCE AND CO-CREATE WEALTH BY BEING A DANCING PARTNER OF UNIVERSE.

11:11

ONE WORLD

ONE DREAM

ONE CONSCIOUNESS

ONE LOVE

Contents

Contents

Foreword

KINJAL PRAKASH PANCHOLI, the author of this book has had 19 years of turbulent life journey which he had to undergo as it was part of his Soul Journey which he never realised till Covid-19 Pandemic. This house arrest due to Lockdown where he didn't have any option except for understanding the mysteries of Universe as his Spirit Guides never left his side until he understood the Laws of Universe and made him experience the mysterious ways of how Abundance and Manifestations worked and being a curious learner he always questioned the laws but that was what I guess Universe loved him as he was a very stubborn person and never accepted any practices or laws of his own or other religions as it is, and also Education system or any Famous Guru or Institutions unless he was covinced the logic or practical implementaion in our Daily Personal Life. He never accepted any Laws of Universe as well until he was covinced with the understanding of the law. He has had life journey of 39 years with the graph where he saw victories after perseverence and also riches from family and also life breakdown with his education at Stake where he lost his Father and all his properties to Bank Mortgage and also creditors leading the family to court as his father, a tax practitioner lost all the wealth due to Share Speculation and was heavily indebted to both banks and private lenders. He was an extremely inteligent student and a balanced person who never left any goals midway no matter what obstacles come his way, he will make his way out and give his best. He is a Phoenix who surely knows how to Rise from Ashes. He will never quit like any normal human being would have. He studied for his Chartered

Accountancy final exams (which is the toughest exam to pass in first attempt as only 2 to 3 percent people would pass the exams in entire India) in the Criminal Court as his father had opened an investment firm in his name while he was a minor and his father had the Cheques signing authority to pay Stock Broker. He went through a period of DOOM as he lost his father, his family without any shelter and no riches, and to top it his final CA exams were due. The stress does not end here, the stock broker had bounced the cheques which his father had signed for his Investment Firm and the broker files a Criminal Case of Cheque bouncing which Kinjal had to inadvertently face with a warrant from Police Station and to add to stress levels he had to attend court alone and take his CA Final books to the court every 15 days and study in the Trial Room of Court. No Father, No House, Inherited Liabilities, No money for house rent or food and to add to misery hire a lawyer to fight the case and pressure to pass the CA exams as he had no other option. Miracle happend that he passed the exams first attempt despite Do or Die Situation. After 2 years of trials he had to pay dues for closing the case with Zero fault of his and no Inheritnace nor he had begun earning. His Journey of Phoenix begins here as he sought a way out for any situation and also emerged a winner with excellency and managed Education, Debts, Court Trails, with No Father and No House. He still decides to go to UK for his MBA studies. After such a troublesome life this move of his required guts but he achieved it and came back to India as there was recession in 2008 due to Sub prime mortgage crises with no job at hand and education debt to deal with. Again a setback, which put his hopes down to level 2 from level 1 before. But he uses his skills of a Phoenix and pays off the loan at the time of crisis and buys a house and gets married and sets up factory for waste management for around 1 million USD. His marriage was like a fairy tale wedding of top celebrities and a lovely house and promising factor. But after 5 years of marriage he falls to pit to a Level which is unimaginable. Guess what, he again lost his house, marriage failed and business didnt work. Third wave of shock in life at Personal and Financial level. But he decides to fight back again and with No penny he still finds a way to Survive with a Smiling Face. He succeded again but to know how will be a question for all of us. UNIVERSE lifts him up from the pitfall and gifts him the Laws of Universe and how he felt the prescence of Invisible forces like Angels, Ascended Masters, His Ancestors and His Animal Spirit Guides cheered him by making him beleive another world which he never heard, never seen or never been taught or felt. During Pandemic, these invisible Divine forces came to his rescue by making hime feel secure and convinced him that his soul chose to evolve in this period of 19 years which was the most dangerous period as growing big 3 times and falling 3 times will make any normal person reach a level of Insanity or Suicidal. No career, No House, and a Divorce plus Pandemic. but little did he know that these 2 years of transformation from being a caterpillar to a butterfly would give him this Magical powers and knowledge to Align with Frequency of Abundance by learning manisfestation skills at a small and later he started manifesting small things instantly and his Guides never let him down. He chose to take FAITH in Quantum Physics. Manifestation of our desires arise in our thoughts and Inner eye chakra through visualisations and exist in Parallel Universe and come to our reality once we raise our vibrational frequency from. His Guides helped him by showing these magical signs and communicated via numbers to give him confidence to understand whether his manifestations were closeby and answered all his questions for his Past Trauma and his Past lives are not failures but Soul Lessons to evolve to being Master Manifestor and see magic in his Life. He was so overwhelmed to see these signs from the Universe and his spirit guides through Car License plates, Animals , You tube Videos, Emails from Cosmos and via People. His life felt magical at the time of Covid-19 as he was convinced his Guides protected him for Covid-19 crisis as his Residence building had covid virus on all the floors except for his floor and his neighbours on the same floor of his can vouch for that. His leap of faith on Universe in Pandemic, made him understand no theory but practical and all happening in front of his eyes on Road , Mother Nature, Airports, You tube, Emails and got answers from these loving invisible forces who helped him metamorphose and see manisfestations happening instantaneously as in Quantum Physics, if we are a vibrational match to the frequency of abundance by Collapsing Time and Space, which is effortless and that is the Power of Human Mind. But to experience this magic entire Humanity whether rich or poor can manifest love, wealth, health, and anything once they follow the tools mnetioned by him during the course of this book. Just academic understanding and not practically applying the readers of this book will not experience this manifestation magic unless they have faith like the author kept and practiced and understood all the chapters with physically seeing in the Our Physical World. I believe him as his practice tools and wisdom from Spirit Guides mentioned in this book has made me feel and see my frequency rising. This Divine wisdom he wishes to gift and share with the entire Humanity, as reality we see is an illusion and we all can become abundant and feel high vibrations. His mother always mentioned that he was a blessed divine child who was born to share his Divine Light and Wisdom to entire Human Life as his trials nand tribulations are an Inspiration to entire population on the planet as **One Should Never Quit , Universe has Got Your Back**. Take a leap of faith by dropping our egos and listen to our Intuitional Inner Voice of Heart and Soul by eliminationg the garbage from our conscious mind by rewiring our sub conscious mind , working on our Body and Soul. Once we align with the energies of Universe , the MAGIC IS ALL AROUND. He mentions SEE IT to BELIEVE IT.

- Rajneesh Duggal 2022

Preface

The primary objective of the book is to uplift Humanity and help them discover their Soul Purpose for which they incarnated on the Planet Earth as per their Soul Contracts by introducing tools through which they remain in Higher Vibrations and dissolve the EGO of their mind and listen to their Hearts for following their Soul Path to align with the abundant frequency of the Universe. Currently, Humanity is leading a life of Duality thereby staying at lower vibrations and misaligned with the energy of abundance and leading to massive destruction of all life forms on the planet. The best part of the book is that each of us on this planet has Universe and its team to help us discover our Soul Path and effortlessly attract Abundance which we should claim as Our Birth Right. Universe will never let you quit and it wants to give you all luxuries but we are not in that frequency. Just like a Radio Channel at frequency of 98.3 FM will let you listen to song clearly, but moment it is at any other frequency we will have disturbance while listening. UNIVERSE HAS ALWAYS GOT YOUR BACK and it will keep speaking to you through the language of numbers and other magical signs to give you abundance and wealth but we don't listen as it requires awareness and being in the present to interpret. It will not let you fail but one should have faith as there is no coincidence on this Planet. Author has experienced the support from Universe and never quit for 19 years of his Struggle and experiencing magic during pandemic. He wants to INSPIRE Humanity that once we understand our failures which won't be failures anymore as they will turn into lessons for which our Soul has decided before incarnation and signed a Soul

Contract with Universe. So abundance is not for only one percent population, it is the birth right of every Human Being as Universe wants to give but we should be ready to claim. Dance with the Universe as it has come MIDWAY to give our desired abundance but we as the better half of Dancing Couple Partner are not claiming it.

BELIEVE & MANIFEST and be the LIGHT FOR ABUNDANCE AS A CO-CREATOR WITH DANCING PARTNER UNIVERSE

Acknowledgements

*"BEING GRATEFUL IS THE HIGHEST LEVEL OF
VIBRATIONAL TOOL FOR ALIGNING WITH THE
FREQUENCY OF ABUNDANCE "*
I AM GRATITUDE
I BREATHE GRATITUDE
I LIVE GRATITUDE
I FEEL GRATITUDE
I DREAM & SLEEP GRATITUDE
<u>*FOR*</u>
SOURCE : ALMIGHTY : CREATOR : GOD
UNIVERSE
MOTHER GAIA EARTH
MY LOVING PARENTS & FAMILY
MY SPIRIT TEAM OF ARCHANGELS, ASCENDED
MASTERS, ANCESTORS & SPIRIT ANIMAL TOTEMS
ALL MY LOVED ONES & FRIENDS
MY TEACHERS
MOTHER NATURE , SUN, MOON, WATER, PLANTS
& TREES, WATER
ENTIRE COSMOS COMPRISING OTHER PLANETS,
STARS & GALAXIES
MUSIC, DANCE (MY PASSION)
MY BODY PARTS EYES, EARS, HANDS & LEGS,
NOSE, LUNGS, HEART, KIDNEY, BRAIN, AND ALL MY
CELLS
FOR EACH DAY I LIVE, OXYGEN I BREATHE AND
LOVE I FEEL
AND TO EACHONE & EVERYTHING I MISSED
NAMING ABOVE WHOM & WHICH HAVE MADE ME
WHAT I AM TODAY

ACKNOWLEDGEMENTS

* I AM SORRY*
* PLEASE FORGIVE ME*
I THANK YOU
I LOVE YOU
FOR EVERY SECOND OF MY LIFE

CHAPTER ONE

Signs from Universe & How to Interpret them ?

UNIVERSE MIRRORS YOUR DESIRES & THOUGHTS IN THE INFINITE FIELD OF CONSCIOUSNESS

&

THEN WE MANIFEST IN OUR REALITY

Let us suppose, you're planning a trip, but you can't decide between a secluded mountain retreat, or a week on the beach. Then, everywhere you go, you see pictures of the ocean, whales, boats, and you notice beach towels are on sale at the store. Or, you're reading a book, and suddenly find yourself in a beach scene...

Gee, I wonder where you should go on your vacay?

THIS IS A SIGN from the Universe. Actually, multiple signs, but you get what I'm saying.

The Universe WANTS you to be happy, I promise. It will gently guide you to make choices that are in your highest good, and that guidance can feel really good... or not so good.

Maybe you're at a job you don't like, and things keep going wrong. You get passed up for all the promotions. You can't seem to clock in on time. You continually spill coffee on your shirt.

It could even transfer to your personal life, making dating difficult, your car is always breaking down, or you can't seem to kick that cold you've been fighting for weeks.

The Universe is telling you that you are in the wrong job!

In short, the easy way to know if you're doing well, is if the Universe keeps sending you good stuff, and if you're not... I mean...DUH. You may have a weird rash that just won't go away.

Pythagoras stated that our universe is ruled by numbers, and everything is mathematically precise. Numbers are a universal language, and can show up to give us messages, especially when they come in repeated sequence, such as 111, 222, 333, and so on, and most especially if you keep seeing the same sequence over and over.

Number signs can be seen on a clock, an odometer, a street address, anything! As far as what they mean? Well, numerology definitely plays a part here, but remember, go with what resonates with YOU, not necessarily what someone else says.

BE PRESENT & BE AWARE

Numbers & Signs is the Language of Universe

While a double number is significant, when the same number is tripled or quadrupled, or more, it means that the message is that much stronger, so pay heed. If you see more than four of the same number in a row, the Universe is really trying to get your attention!

Here are a few messages that numbers could be bringing to you, but remember to always take what resonates and leave the rest. (For example, if the sequence "649" means something to you personally, and you keep seeing it in random places, then it's a sign!)

1111 has recently been assigned to signify that you're on a spiritual path of enlightenment. It's also called an "Angel Number," which we'll get to in the next section.

22, 222 or 2222: While "22" is a Master Builder number, a triple or quad "2" means that a new cycle is about to start that will bring growth and expansion into your life. Also, balance, call to action, love/romance, and union.

33, 333 or 3333: Seeing this sequence will align you with your path, if you've strayed a bit, and also means divine union, oneness, truth, and your spiritual gifts are awakening.

44, 444 or 4444: This can mean that someone is trying to communicate with you, either in the physical world or from the other side. It also reminds you that your guides are by your side always. It can also signify balance, harmony, organization, perfection, and justice.

It can also mean that you are at a very significant turning point about a major decision in your life and that you'll soon see amazing results from all of the hard work you have been doing.

55, 555 or 5555: This number sequence means CHANGE. Big changes are coming your way if you keep seeing this. It may be telling you that it's time to surrender to the ebb and flow of the Universe, allow it to remove things from your life, to make room for something new. Trust the process.

66, 666, or 6666: No, this sequence is not evil. Quite the contrary. Repeating 6's signifies family, that you either need to foster deeper family relationships, or that you already have them, and you should allow yourself to lean on them during hard times.

It can also be telling you that something in your life is dying. But don't worry, it's something that is no longer serving you, so let it go.

77, 777, or 7777: You have a message to share with the world, either through writing, music, or art. This number represents collective consciousness, spiritual enlightenment and spiritual awakening. This number is also about spiritual acceptance and growth. Expect miracles in your life.

88, 888, or 8888: This number repeated is a sign of balance and abundance in friends and family, or money. Also means infinity, or a never-ending cycle (one you may need to break...?), duality, or "as above, so below."

99, 999, or 9999: This number means the current path in your life is about to come to an end. This does not mean death, but that your life is about to shift and get a whole lot better. Also, it can mean forgiveness and that you're ready to be the real YOU or trust the plan the Universe has for you.

10, or 1010: This means completion. A cycle has ended and a new one can now begin. It is the number of universal creation, and signifies having faith in yourself and your ability to be the creator of your own life.

CHAPTER THREE

What are Angel Numbers ?

Angel Numbers" is the name given to synchronicities and signs that come through repeating numbers and are said to be from your angel guides, or the angelic realm. EVERYONE has at least one angelic guide, so the source of the message is believed to be amplified coming directly from an angelic being.

1s: A reset or starting something new. The beginning.

2s: Harmony, either internal or external, or both. Go within and balance your energy.

3s: In triplicate, this number represents the essence of the trinity, mind, body, spirit.

4s: Trust your wisdom and your psychic powers, and you will be able to trust yourself.

5s: Change is coming, be open for anything.

6s: Focus on family, balancing work and homelife.

7s: Good things are coming! Trust your instincts and your angelic guides.

8s: Abundance, wealth, money, and good fortune are in store for you!

9s: Something is ending, so you can find and embrace your true passion

10s: Trust that you are on the right path.

When you see Angel Numbers on a daily basis, your angels are definitely talking to you, pulling for you, and guiding you on your path! Don't forget to thank them for these Heavenly messages!

CHAPTER FOUR

Signs In Dreams

In the dreamscape, our resistant, day-to-day "monkey mind" is asleep, making room for the Higher Self to take the wheel of our consciousness. We are much more open to receiving messages in this state.

Many complain about not remembering dreams, but the thing to focus on is the feeling you have upon waking. The feeling is the important part, for in the feeling, the emotion, is the message and it's for you to decipher.

A happy dream will likely leave you with a good feeling when you wake up and may hold the message that you're on the right track, or confirmation of a recent decision, or even just a reconnection with a loved one who wants to say hi. These are wonderful and give us motivation, hope, and the confidence to keep moving forward.

Other types of messages can come through dreams that aren't so warm and fuzzy... like nightmares. A bad dream can make you feel uneasy, sad, or afraid. The emotion you feel, if you have no other memory of the dream, is the thing your guidance is trying to show you.

What have you been afraid of in your life, or what (or who?) makes you uneasy? If you're afraid of taking a leap of faith, a dream that makes you fearful may be trying to show you that it's time to jump, for example.

If you wake up sad, explore what is coming up in the waking world that is dragging your vibration down. Chances are, it's ready to be released.

A dream that shows you a person you may know doing bad things is likely a message that you do not need that person in your life.

There are a plethora of books out there that might help, but, ultimately, YOU are the best judge of what your dreams mean. After all, a bear in your dream could mean abundance to you, while it might mean danger to someone else.

Although dreams can seem very encrypted at times. your guides will try to communicate with you through things that resonate on a personal level. Your favorite animals, foods, movies, cars, movie stars, etc, may show up in dreams to help you interpret them.

Having trouble remembering your dreams? A dream journal, kept right next to your bed, can be handy, and those who use one regularly even experience increased remembering over time.

Train yourself to reach for that journal immediately when you wake up. Write down what you felt, everything you remember, and you may find that more of the dream returns.

Some believe that every single dream you have holds significance, a sign or a message of some sort. From whence this guidance comes is a matter of personal opinion, but the fact that nearly everyone has a story about receiving divine guidance while they're in dreamland is proof enough that it's not just a fluke.

Authors talk about dreaming their next best-sellers all the time, and inventors throughout history have noted that they see their next invention, complete and functioning, in their dreams before they've even had the idea for them in the waking world.

More common signs in dreams are those who see the house they will live in or the person they'll eventually be happily married to before they've even caught a glimmer of these things in real life.

Signs in dreams come even when we don't consciously ask for them.

So, imagine the guidance you could receive if you set the intention before you go to sleep every night? The results could be phenomenal.

Don't be afraid to get specific, but be ready to use your detective skills to understand the message that comes through.

CHAPTER FIVE

Deja Vu

We've all heard the term. We've all used it, because we've all experienced it at one time or another in our lives. But what does it REALLY mean?

Usually triggered by something specific, Deja Vu happens when you suddenly feel like you've lived the moment you're in before, down to every detail.

And it doesn't have to be a profound activity to qualify as a legitimate Deja Vu occurrence. It can be as simple as sitting at your dining room table talking to a friend on the phone.

Out of nowhere, you get the strange feeling that you've been there before, done that very thing before, in exactly the same way, and you're not sure if it's because you actually HAVE, or if it's a glitch in the Matrix.

Some believe this sensation is because you've just tapped into your well of infinite knowledge, and, if you also have the belief that you had a hand in writing your life before you began living it, down to the detail, that you simply "remembered" writing it.

I've always liked that explanation. It gave meaning to something that no one else could explain the first time it happened to me. But, I think I've got a better definition.

Deja Vu is a sign, a message from your guides that you are on the right track. A signal to keep going. It's an encouraging pat on the back that you're doing it, and they're rooting for you!

Imagine you're running your first marathon, and your guides are on the sidelines, screaming and cheering you on. You may be tired, frustrated, maybe your knee hurts, and you're thinking of quitting.

Then, you hear your guides before you see them, because, let's face it, Archangel Michael is LOUD and can do that ear-piercing whistle thing where you put your fingers in your mouth, and then you see them, all jumping up and down and yelling and grinning at you.

They KNOW you can do this, and they're going to be by your side every step of the way, encouraging you to keep going, and reminding you that what you've been working toward is just around the corner.

CHAPTER SIX

Messages in Music

It's no secret that music has a profound effect on us. The frequencies of sound can elicit strong emotions, especially specific songs we hear during powerful events in our life. From that day forward, hearing the song brings back the energy and emotion of the event.

This can be a good, or bad thing.

Our guides love to use music as a vehicle for messages, too.

Have you ever noticed that songs will play on the radio while you're in your car that match how you're feeling? Or make you feel better about a situation because just the right song comes on? Or you think about someone and a song comes on that reminds you of them?

This is no coincidence.

It's a sign!

If you start to pay close attention to the music around you, I guarantee you'll start hearing the synchronicities and messages.

A song that won't get out of your head likely contains some hidden meaning that could help you along your path right now, as would a song that is already playing in your mind when you wake up.

Signs through music are often accompanied by other synchronicities, like repeated numbers. A song plays, it elicits an emotion because you resonate with it for some reason, and then you notice the time on the clock is 2:22 PM.

That's a confirmation that the song DOES hold a message for you, so don't write it off as chance!

Only YOU know what the messages are, and what they mean, so don't let anyone else tell you differently.

For example, you may hear a song you and your ex used to listen to, and every time you hear it, you feel sad. But for some reason, this time, it makes you feel really good, because it reminds you that you broke free from that toxic relationship, and it gives you a renewed feeling of empowerment in your own life.

Don't overanalyze it! Never resist a positive message! And trust your instincts. Usually, your first inkling is the right one.

Getting messages through music has got to be the most fun way to receive guidance, don't you think? And singing raises your vibration, so go ahead, sing along!

I always listened to the song "Work Bitch" by Britney Spears which motivated me every morning that if I wanted Lamborghini, Big Mansion, Party In France, Never Quit in Life, Just be the Champion, Holding Your Fingers Up to the Sky and etc. to bring Abundance in Life which was an Encouragement Sign as it was dedicated from my guides and angels which always played on my phone unknowingly.

CHAPTER SEVEN

How Gaia & Animals Deliver Messages to Us

We ALL have animal guides, whether you've connected to yours yet or not. Animals are direct line to Gaia, Mother Earth, the planet we live on and depend on, and they will often arrive with important signs to keep us on moving forward on our paths.

Like a lot of our guides, animal "spirit guides" can come and go as we need them, but we do tend to have a few permanent creatures that are always with us.

Think of the one or two animals you just can't get enough of, or that will ALWAYS make you stop scrolling on Facebook. Yep, chances are, those would be your main animal guides.

So, how do they deliver messages to us, and how do we KNOW they do this?

The Native Americans have always had a deep connection to animals, and their various cultures are all filled with examples of animal totems and symbolism, but they aren't the only ones who have ever turned to the wild for guidance.

When the Universe puts an animal in your path, pay attention. What were you thinking about when you saw it?

Repetitive sightings of the same animal is definitely a message from your guides, and most likely one that has a personal meaning for you, based on what type of animal you see.

If the animal itself has no special meaning for you, don't fret. They do tend to bring the same message to everyone. Here are a few examples:

Hawk - a powerful messenger of the spirit world, the hawk wants you to "see" something more clearly. In other words, trust your inner "sight," or your intuition in a matter that may be plaguing you. The hawk may also be telling you to try to see something from a higher perspective.

Crow - Associated with magic, wisdom and mystery, the crow symbolizes destiny, intelligence and powerful creation. In a positive sense, the crow can appear as a sign of personal transformation and good fortune, reminding you that magic is all around you.

Deer - A gentle but strong creature, the deer shows you how to navigate obstacles in your path with speed and agility. It is associated with love, compassion and giving, and can bring the message of innocence, reminding you to reconnect with your inner child.

Dragonfly - Seeing a dragonfly means that you have guides from the fairy realm! It is a message of happiness, representing joy and lightness, and also transformation. Call on the dragonfly energy if you feel you are going through significant spiritual changes.

Fox - Usually associated with trickery, this cunning animal also symbolizes quick thinking and adaptability. A fox sighting may be telling you to expand your perspective and try a new approach.

Butterfly - get ready for big change, because the butterfly practically SCREAMS metamorphosis. You may be coming out of a hermiting phase or personal transformation, but now you're ready to spread your new wings and fly!

Now, you don't have to see these animals in person to receive a message. A picture on the internet, a billboard, or the subway counts! They can also show up on jewelry, paintings, clothing, just about anything!

An important note, animals will never bring a message of doom, but rather, how to navigate through whatever it is that you're in the thick of. It's vital that you see every sighting, even one you wouldn't normally welcome, as divine guidance.

And yes, that includes spiders in your house. Be calm and open, allow your intuition to tell you what the message is that the little guy is trying to convey, and then let him go on his merry way... OUTSIDE.

Spiders get a bad rap. They are just as spiritual as dragonflies and butterflies, and can bring very important messages, such as a mysterious adventure on the horizon for you. They can also provide support and a "Keep going, you got this!" cheer if you're in the midst of some serious spiritual growth.

CHAPTER EIGHT

Signs During Meditation

Meditation is vital as part of a spiritual practice, but it's not as easy as it looks. The rule used to be "quiet your mind," but when you're learning to meditate, that seems like an impossible task.

Focusing on a clear mind can drive you bonkers, so, instead, just sit in a quiet space and BE. You must allow the thoughts from your day to swirl around in your head until they swirl themselves out. They will, don't worry. It may take half an hour, but they will.

You'll notice that the time it takes for the monkey mind to call "Uncle!" is less and less each time you try, if you're consistent. If you're new to meditation, make a point to sit and BE for at least 10 minutes a day.

Be mindful of what comes up in your thoughts, because they could also be signs of things that need attention.

Much like the sleep state, when we're in a calm, meditative place, we open ourselves up to receiving messages from our guides much easier. And they know it.

If you just can't seem to stay mindful of your breathing because you keep thinking about a coworker, chances are, there is something about that person that you need to be aware of. It could be a sign that you need to release them from your energy, or that you may have a connection with them that one, or both of you, is denying.

You can also set an intention during meditation to receive a sign or guidance on something specific, so don't be shy. As you're assuming the "criss cross applesauce" position, ask for direction!

Meditation is traditionally used to calm the mind, body and spirit, and it's just a good idea to make it part of your daily routine.

CHAPTER NINE

Your Body is Talking to You

There are four main energy bodies, physical, mental, emotional, and spiritual. It's important to take care of all of them.

When we neglect one, it lets us know in some way. The physical body is very skilled at this, but we tend to ignore the signs from it more than the others.

It's somehow easier for us to meet the needs of the other three bodies. When the emotional body needs a purge, we cry. When the mental body needs a break, we take a bath, curl up with a good book, or take a walk. When the spiritual body needs attention, we meditate.

But, humans have a knack for pressing on with their day through physical discomfort, and put off addressing it. The physical body is literally the vessel we chose to live this life in, and yet, it ends up last on our to-do list.

Those aches and pains are likely trying to tell you something. Signs that your body is trying to communicate with you can come in various ways, like the aforementioned mystery aches and pains, fatigue, nausea, insomnia, no appetite, sickness, or pain that isn't a mystery.

For example, if you know your posture at your desk can slump, and that causes lower back pain, and your lower back is hurting... well... that doesn't take a brain surgeon to figure out what's going on. Additionally, if you keep getting sick, maybe it's time to change your diet.

Those types of messages are easy, because they remind you to address immediate issues that go away with some relatively straightforward measures.

Other signals your body is sending you may not be so cut and dry. Because all the energy bodies are interconnected, one flowing seamlessly into the next, emotional blocks can manifest into physical discomfort if not dealt with, and will only get worse the longer you let them go.

The physical body is very smart, and is designed for self-preservation. It wants to be healthy, and when it's lacking, it sends you a message.

A consistently tight hip could indicate a toxic relationship that is begging to be healed, or an abandonment issue from the past that you need to release.

A simple way to figure out what, exactly, you have buried in aching parts of your physical body is to take note of what you were thinking about when the pain started and see if there's a correlation with the thoughts when the pain returns. Once you have that, it's just a matter of running it through whatever healing modality works for you.

The important thing is to pay attention to the needs of ALL your energy bodies, and give them what they need before a physical condition becomes chronic.

CHAPTER TEN

The Universe Speaks to Us Through Tech

You've probably figured out by now that the Universe can send us messages in pretty much any form it wants, anything that will get our attention. And if we continue to ignore them, they up the ante, making the signs bigger, more elaborate... more painful.

Because we spend so much of our waking time on our phones, computers, tablets and televisions, one way we can receive messages is through our technical devices.

Have you ever been thinking about someone and then suddenly they call or text you? This is just one example.

Other messages through tech are synchronicities through television shows, commercials, Facebook ads, or even someone else's feed on social media.

Maybe you need advice on a looming decision, and someone randomly posts something that unwittingly provides that advice. Or, you're contemplating a move, and you come across a "Best Places to Live" article.

Or, you want to change jobs, and a friend posts about his company opening up in your area.

Tech can also glitch, turn off and on, open or close windows you didn't click on, show you pictures you don't remember taking, and so on. These types of signs usually have a very personal significance that only you can decipher.

CHAPTER ELEVEN

How to See Signs and Use Them for Your Benefits

How do we start to SEE the signs the Universe is throwing at us 24/7?

Well, start paying attention, and know that there are no coincidences, only synchronicities, and you'll see messages everywhere. And the more you believe, the more you'll see, and so on and so forth.

What you really need to embrace is that signs can be ANYTHING and come from ANYWHERE. Your guides know what will resonate with you, and you alone, and therefore, tailor the messages they send.

Don't worry, they won't give up. They'll keep firing signs and messages at you until you see them, because it's their job. And your guides take their job VERY seriously.

Once you start seeing the signs, you can use them to either alter your course, or stay steady, and things will start to fall into place.

It takes a commitment from you to make a change, if necessary. If you're not willing to make that change, then the signs may become more and more uncomfortable in your life.

If you keep getting hints that you need to leave your job, but you're too afraid, the messages will get more frequent, and may even culminate in you being fired. Although this does the trick, obviously, it's not ideal.

Sometimes, we're asked to do something that is outside our comfort zone, and the signs are undeniable. These situations are incredible opportunities to grow, so close your eyes and jump. You won't be sorry.

Your guides will never get angry with you for not seeing the signs they so painstakingly devise, but they will cheer and celebrate with you when you see one and use it to make your life better. They're like besties that way.

CHAPTER TWELVE

What Happens When You Ignore the Signs?

Just in case you haven't gotten the gist of this yet, I'll spell it out for you...

When you ignore the signs, they'll get bigger, stronger, more uncomfortable, more disruptive, and include things like illness, accidents, being fired from your job, or being so entangled in a toxic relationship that it just gets harder and harder to walk away the longer you wait.

Don't ignore the signs. Just. Don't

CHAPTER THIRTEEN

High Vibrational Divine Daily Practices to Attract Abundance in Our Life

We live in a Friendly Universe and it wants us to help attract and manifest Abundance in all areas of life like:

Finance and Career

Relationships and Love

Health

Spirituality for the Growth of our Soul

It is our birth right to live with Abundance and

Co-Create with the Light: Source: Universe.

The basic divine spiritual practices to follow is to remain in Higher Vibrations so that We are in Alignment with the Frequency of Abundance of Universe. Once we start moving towards the Higher Vibrations, Abundance flows naturally to us Effortlessly. We start connecting with the Magical Signs and Numbers of the Universe which Guides us on Daily Basis . But the

THUMBRULE

"WE MUST KEEP FAITH & BE IN PRESENT WITH AWARENESS"

The practices we must follow daily to keep us in Higher Vibrations are

Practice Gratitude

Meditation

Self Love

Listening to Music, Dance and following our Passion and Hobbies

Exercising and Stretching our Body

Ho'oponopono Prayer

Breathing Exercises to let Life Force Energy IN

Walking Barefooted on Mother Earth, Grass, Sand on the Beach

Practice Gratitude

We should be grateful to Universe and Mother Gaia Earth for providing us with basic things, living creature sent in our lifes and Mother Nature for keeping us Alive and Breathe in Light daily to keep us Happy, Joyous and Abundant.

Tip: Write down 50 to 100 Gratitude Affirmations in the Journal or record the audio in our own voice or surf through Youtube videos and listen to them or speak out Loud or in our mind , moment we get up in the Morning for atleast 10 minutes.

Be GRATEFUL for the *New Day in our Life and *Oxygen which we are provided free of cost as that is our Basic & Most Important Necessity of Life for which we don't have to spend a single penny as this is the most taken for granted aspect of Life for which we as Human Beings Neglect as the Creator didn't charge us for. We realised during PANDEMIC that how Vital Oxygen was as there were Countless Deaths due to Absence of Oxygen which even MONEY COULDN'T BUY. These are small things for us as were provided for free and we should Praise the Lord for not burdening us to buy which we simply NEGLECT.

"I remeber reading an Article in The Newspaper where a Billionaire in Europe died of Lack of Oxygen and his daughter mentioned that her father instructed to throw all the MONEY on STREETS as his LIFE TIME EARNINGS

WAS VALUELESS." Lets practice gratitude for every breath we take and new day in our life, this lets us to be in surrender mode and brings Vibrations of the Highest Frequency to Attract Abundance. Its like a radio channel if not tuned to 98.3 FM it will not align with best sound frequency mode and there will be disturbance and irritation to listen to the music.

My 50 Gratitude Affirmations can be used for Daily Practices especially in the Morning once you wake up and read them aloud/silently :

1. Thank you for God for the New Day in my Life
2. Thank you for Mother Nature
3. Thank you for Oxygen
4. Thank you for the ability to Love and Being Loved
5. Thank you for my eyes for ability to see such beautiful things God has made
6. Thank you for my legs to walk in the places where I feel wonderful
7. Thank you for my hands to eat food and hold things
8. Thank you for my brain, lungs, heart, kidney and internal organs to make my body function well
9. Thank you for my ears to hear
10. Thank you for my skin and cells to protect me
11. Thank you for Sun
12. Thank you for Moon
13. Thank you for Stars
14. Thank you for all planets and galaxies
15. Thank you for my lovely Parents
16. Thank you for Family

17.   Thank you for Teachers who made me wise and knowledgable

18.   Thank you for Friends

19.   Thank you for Work and Career

20.   Thank you for my finances, savings and investments

21.   Thank you for Music

22.   Thank you for Dance

23.   Thank you for my ability to comprehend things in life

24.   Thank you for my reasoning

25.   Thank you for my answers

26.   Thank you for school, college and higher studies

27.   Thank you for divine wisdom

28.   Thank you for Roof over my head

29.   Thank you for Night Sky

30.   Thank you for my book publishing

31.   Thank you for my ability to speak

32.   Thank you for my shower

33.   Thank you for all scientists, inventors, techies, authors, academicians etc

34.   Thank you for divine spot in me

35.   Thank you for my ability to touch and be touched

36.   Thank you for night sky

37.   Thank you for smell

38.   Thank you for water

39.   Thank you for plants

40.   Thank you for cats, dogs, birds and all other animals

41.   Thank you for my clothes

42.   Thank you for food

43.   Thank you for transportation

44.   Thank you for my car

45.   Thank you for my abilty to write

46.   Thank you for my Angels, Ascended Masters,
Ancestors and Spirit Animal for guiding me

47.   Thank you for everything and everyone whom I didn't
mention above

48.   Thank you once again for New Day

49.   Thank you once again for oxygen

50.   Thank you once again for Mother Nature

Meditation & Awareness by Being in the Present Moment

Meditation is the most misunderstood term and everyone refrains from doing it as it is perceived to avoid thoughts while remaing silent and I agree thats the toughest thing to do.

But its not what it is perceived, and infact please sit with eyes closed and most importantly spine erect and observe the thoughts which come and especially the stillness between two thoughts. Please welcome all thoughts (when you meditate for atleast 10 to 15 minutes daily) and allow mind to do that , since mind does always the opposite, slowly you will observe the thoughts escaping or becoming lesser and then you feel the SERENITY & BLISSFULNESS. Sitting erect with Closed Eyes and Observing the stillness between two thoughts will make you feel calmer and also increase your awareness by remaining in the Power of Now or Present. Practice daily as there is No Right or Wrong way of doing but practice will make you understand the benefits of your day going very smoothly and 10 minutes of meditation equals to 2 hours of sleep.

Meditation will by itself keep your level of consciouness high and you will keep vibrations higher as you learn to remain in the PRESENT and BEING AWARE. Keep an alarm every 2 hours in mobile with a reminder of being aware so that you will tune into correcting your thoughts if they are oscillating between Past or Future. Being Aware of your thoughts each second is the best way to keep high vibrations.

SELF LOVE

"I AM " AFFIRMATIONS practiced veryday morning, evening or in our mind even when we take a break blossoms our Heart and Soul to be in the Highest Frequency to Align with the Abundant Energy of the Universe.

Learn to Love Yourself and Read atleast 50 "I AM" SELF LOVE Affirmations during the day or after shower as Loving yourself is Not Being Selfish , Only when you love yourselves you will love others as an Empty Jug can quench thirst of None.

My recommended 50 affirmations:

1. I LOVE MYSELF
2. I AM PRECIOUS
3. I RADIATE BEAUTY
4. I AM HAPPY FROM WITHIN
5. MY HEART IS AT PEACE
6. I AM CONTENT
7. I MATTER
8. I AM ENOUGH
9. I RADIATE SELF CONFIDENCE
10. I ACKNOWLEDGE MY SELF WORTH
11. MY SELF ESTEEEM IS GROWING DAY BY DAY
12. I AM COURAGEOUS
13. I AM JOYOUS
14. I AM BLESSED
15. I AM ALIGNED WITH MY HIGHER CONSCIOUNESS

16.   I TRUST MY INTUITION

17.   I TREASURE MYSELF

18.   I FEEL GOOD ABOUT MYSELF

19.   I LOVE MY BODY

20.   I NOURISH MY BODY WITH HEALTHY FOOD

21.   I NOURISH MY MIND WITH POSITIVE THOUGHTS

22.   I ACCEPT COMPLIMENTS EASILY

23.   I RADIATE LOVE

24.   I DESERVE LOVE

25.   I ATTRACT LOVE

26.   I AM LOVED

27.   I BELIEVE IN MY ABILITIES TO SUCCEED

28.   I FOLLOW MY DREAM

29.   I WELCOME SUCCESS

30.   I DO MY BEST

31.   I ATTRACT WONDERFUL THINGS IN MY LIFE

32.   I AM FULL OF LIFE

33.   I ACCEPT & ACKNOWLEDGE MY EMOTIONS

34.   I AM PERFECT THE WAY I AM

35.   I FORGIVE MYSELF

36.   I MAKE A POSITIVE DIFFERENCE IN THE WORLD

37.   I AM PROUD OF HOW FAR I HAVE COME

38.   I HONOUR MY LIFE PATH

39.   I HAVE THE POWER TO CHANGE

40.   I HONOUR THE OPPORTUNITIES I RECEIVE

41.   I MAKE THE RIGHT CHOICES

42.   I RESPECT MY OWN BOUNDARIES

43.   I TREAT MYSELF WITH RESPECT

44.   I AM THANKFUL FOR MY ACCOMPLISHMENTS

45.   I AM PROUD OF WHO I AM BECOMING

46.   I AM GRATEFUL FOR WHO I AM

47.   I AM THE HEALER OF MY LIFE

48.   I AM KIND & FORGIVING MYSELF

49.   I VALUE & ACCEPT MYSELF

50.   I AM HEALTHY

Listening to Music, Dance and following our Passion and Hobbies

Music and Dance are the best Meditative Practices for me as I instantly move from crowded thoughts running in my mind to pure blissful and no thought state. As rightly said " SOUND IS THE BEST HEALER". Music is meditative as it ruptures all your negative thoughts and creates a still or no thought mind, effortlessly. Dance while listening to Music transfers the High Vibrations and Good feel factor to all cells of the body.

If all cells of the body dance/vibrate at the same level of energy, there is bound to be High Prana levels and no disease body. DISEASE IS NOTHING BUT *DIS-EASE* OF MIND which requires no Doctor to heal as we ourselves can fight traumatic diseases or don't attract disease if:

OUR MIND IS AT EASE NO MATTER WHAT EXTERNAL CIRCUMSTANCES ARE, BY PRACTICING BEING AN ALCHEMIST AND THEREBY SELF HEALING WITH NO EXTERNAL MEDICAL AID. WE ARE GIFTED BY ALMIGHTY TO HEAL OURSELVES.

Exercising and Stretching our Body

Exercising and Stretching our Body parts creates movement in Non Moving Energy in our body parts which is stagnant by no movement of body parts/cells of the parts. This itself obstructs our manifestations, no matter how hard we train our mind as we are not in sync with our body parts and therby not generating High Vibrations. Sweating and stretching is like applying grease in our body parts to sync and vibrate at Higher Levels.

Ho'oponopono Prayer: SFTL : 4 Magical Words

I AM SORRY

PLEASE FORGIVE ME

I THANK YOU

I LOVE YOU

This is the most Powerful Healing Prayer which one should recite daily 108 times. If time is an issue then make it a habbit to practice it atleast 11 times. Keep a photo of the person in front of you if you want to improve the relationship , if you want to heal financial issues please keep a currency note or coin and then recite, or anything else you want to improve relationship with just imagine that thing or person or keep a photo of that person and then recite the four magical words I mentioned above at least 11 times and if you want to heal faster recite 108 times daily.

This prayer was discovered by Dr Hew Len who could not treat terrorists in his hospital as they didn't allow him to treat them and bit their tongue if he touched them. So he tried to heal them by OWNING RESPONSIBLITY FOR THE TERRORISTS BEHAVIOUR & HEALTH AS HE RIGHTLY SAYS WE ARE ONE CONSCIOUNESS AND BY OWNING THE RESPONIBILITY WE CAN HEAL EACH

OTHER AS WE ARE ONE.

Can you believe all his terrorrist patients got treated without they being touched and within few weeks they got treated and got discharged. This is the MAGIC OF HEALING MONEY OR HEALTH OR RELATIONSHIPS BY RECITING THIS PRAYER OF 4 WORDS WHICH IS THE MOST POWERFUL PRAYER IN THE WORLD.

Breathing Exercises to Let Life Force Energy IN

BREATHING OXYGEN ENABLES US TO INCREASE OUR PRANA LEVEL OF ENERGY WHICH KEEPS US IN THE PRESENT MOMENT IF WE BREATHE AS PER TECHNIQUES MENTIONED BELOW.

Have you ever realised our Emotions control the way we Breathe ? When we are ** SAD/DEPRESSED, our Breathing is Heavy, When we are ** HAPPY our Breathing is Faster and When we are NEUTRAL OR IN THE PRESENT MOMENT, Our Breathing is at Normal State.

Hold your finger and hold it to your nostril and observe the length of your breath and observe the emotion , you will soon realise all emotions have different Breath Lengths.

Techniques of Breathing:

- 369 Breathing: **Breathe In** with a count of 3, then **hold it** for count of 6 times and **Breathe out** through mouth with the count of 9 times
- Breathing in through Left nostril by closing your Right nostril with your Right hand thumb and then close your Left nostril by using your Right hand Middle Finger and vice versa by breathing in through Right

nostril and closing your Left nostril and then breathe out through Left nostril. Repeat it for 15 to 20 counts till you feel your Lungs are expanding and clearing your Nasal Hole.

- Do Sudarshan Kriya by enrolling for Art of Living Happiness programme which can be found online or on website of Art of Living founded by Sri Sri Ravi Shankar. It is blissful as Life force energy that is the Prana Levels of Body go very High which makes you live in present and widespreads your awareness.
- Also do Fire Breathing or pranayam by breathing in and out as fast as possibble by holding your belly out while breathing in and belly in while breathing out. Begin with 80 to 100 counts and increase it to 500 counts slowly and gradually and then after completing counts of fire breaths, breathe in the last count for a longer time and hold it as long as you can and then breathe out. Your upper head will feel no thoughts and timeless and thats the feel which one can use to manifest their desires which should be with an act of gratitude and also with a purpose to give to Humanity.

Please note: Take advice of your medical practitioner if you have any exisitng ailments before using the recommended techniques and do the above for 15 to 20 minutes daily in sequential order or independently or at different intervals of the day.

Walking Barefooted on Grass, Hugging Trees, Lying down on Beach Sand etc

Mother Nature has the Highest Vibrational Energy and by walking barefooted on Grass or Earthy ground, lying down on beach sand or even Hugging a Tree Trunk or Plants will :

TRANSFORM YOUR CURRENT LOW OR NEGATIVE ENERGY LEVEL WITH HIGHEST POSITIVE AND HIGH VIBRATIONAL LEVEL.

CHAPTER FOURTEEN

Low Vibrational Energies which Misaligns us from Abundant Energy

We all as Human Beings usually by default operate at Low Level of Consciousness or Energy since we are always in Ego whether self realised or not. By being indifferent ot intolerable to Religions, Races, Culture, Languages, Countries, Class, Caste we are using Emotions of Hatredness or Revenge or Blame Game or Superiority or Inferiority Complex. At times it is not our fault but being brought up in an environment, family, friends, and peer groups, we cultivate our Sub Conscious Mind which does not let us accept it rationally as EGO is at play. We all know we are Born with No Tags and Die with No Tags, which our Heart ultimately knows the TRUTH but our Mind which is Egoisitic is ALWAYS at Play to Prove Ourself at Individual or Group level or Religion level or Country Level. BEING DUALISITIC IS INHERENT IN US AND THEREBY WE ARE NOT THE TRUTH SEEKERS BY LISTENING TO OUR

HEART AND SOUL WHICH IS THE UTLIMATE DESTINY. BEING TRUE TO OURSELVES WILL MANIFEST TREMENDOUS ABUNDANCE WHICH WE DONT SEEK AT ALL , SO LETS DROP EGO AND BE TRUE TO OURSELVES,

AND

ALIGN WITH ABUNDANCE ENERGY BY BEING ONE PEOPLE, ONE DREAM, ONE CONSCIOUNESS AND ONE WORLD.

SUB CONSCIOUS MIND is THE STEERING WHEEL OF LIFE , left most ignored

Reprogramming our Sub-conscious Mind which instills the Negative Thought Patterns and Unhealed Wounded Energies as a Child instilled by parents, families and friends during the first 10 years after being born is likely to make our Destiny as Sub Conscious Mind is responsible for 80 to 90 percent of our daily thoughts, actions and decisions deeply instilled since childhood and erupt as thoughts at any point of the day that deviates us from our goal and success, career and finance, health and relationships.

No matter How Hard We Try but we don't realise the Source of Our Thoughts which erupt anytime of the day which DEVIATES US FROM OUR DESTINY. By listening to Affirmations, practicing Gratitude, Healing our wounds as a Child, Self Love, and other tools explained in the previous Sub Chapters of High Vibrational Energy Tools will by default reprogramme our Sub-conscious mindset and Ultimately lead us to Achieve our Purpose, Goals and Manifestations which is for OUR HIGHEST GOOD AND ULTIMATELY FOR HIGHEST GOOD OF HUMANITY AND MOTHER GAIA EARTH.

CHAPTER SIXTEEN

FULFILLMENT : THE KEY TO HAPPINESS

MONEY is never Absolute & Always Relative: FULFILLMENT Is Always Absolute

No matter what we manifest be it money, love, health or relations , our Ultimate Source of Being Fulfilled is the Greatest Desire. By achieving the State of Fulfillment we will Never Compare or Relate Ourselves to ANYONE OR ANYTHING. As by always constantly comparing our Material Status or Successes or Achievements or Fame to other people we are in a Constant State of Misery. We as human beings have forgotten WHAT LEADS TO FULFILLMENT and thereby Depressed. Even Richest and Famous people have committed Suicide since they "NEVER FELT ABSOLUTE STATE OF CONTENTMENT, HAPPINESS, PASSIONATE AND FULFILLMENT BY ALWAYS BEING IN STATE OF COMPARISION OR RELATIVENESS NO MATTER WHAT THEY ACHIEVED AT ALL TIMES OF THEIR LIFE".

EQUATION TO HAPPINESS :Which Money Can't Buy Money can Bring Happiness ONLY when we

KNOW *WHERE, *WHEN *WHAT & *WHOM TO SHOP WITH
LET US SELF EVALUATE OURSELVES AND RATE OURSELVES OUT OF 10 IN BELOW MENTIONED 6 ASPECTS OF LIFE

1. MONEY AND CAREER
2. HEALTH
3. FAMILY
4. SPOUSE, LOVE, PARTNER
5. FRIENDS
6. SPIRITUALITY

BY CRITICALLY EVALUATING OURSELVES BY BEING NON-BIASED AND RATE OURSELVES IN ABOVE 6 DIMENSIONS OF LIFE AND BY NUMERICALLY EVEN IF WE SELF RATE => 5/10 IN EACH INDIVIDUAL DIMENSION AND AVERAGE => 6/10 IN ALL 6 DIMENSIONS TOGETHER, I BELIEVE WE HAVE NUMERICALLY ACHIEVED TRUE STATE OF HAPPINESS, SUCCESS, FULFILLMENT AND IN TRUES SENSE ABUNDANCE AND STATE OF ABSOLUTE BLISS IN OUR LIFE.

Authors Smiling Note :

By achieving => 8/10 in average of all 6 dimensions AND failing in one of the six Dimensions individually by being < 5/ 10. (for example by being 3/10 in Health), we have not achieved Success, Abundance and Fulfillment IN TRUE SENSE INTERNALLY even though we might have Monetarily Rated ourselves as 10/10.

US Dollar, Sterling Pounds, Crypto Currencies, Carbon Credit Certificate and You Never Know Future might hold a Currency Note of Abundance

Currency Notes are primafacie basis of an underlying intrinsic value of gold reserves. Might be a futurisitc thinking: a revolution in the future we can have Currency Note of Abundance for each country where underlying value will be gold reserves plus vibrational frequency of Human Population of that Country where a Techgadget can measure Human Body Vibrational Frequency just like Blood Pressure. Currency Note of the country will be Tangible Value of Gold plus Intangible Value by measuring Vibrational Frequency of Human Population of that Country. Since Economy will be valued not only by tangible material, as higher the vibrational frequency of the human population of that Country better will be the Yield for future growth.

This will raise the Vibrational Frequency of the Planet Earth as Human Beings will ascend Spiritually and follow their Soul Path for which their Soul had Contracted before Incarnation.

BEING FUTURISTIC BUT THIS THOUGHT WILL ENABLE THE SOUL GROWTH INDIVIDUALLY AND AT COLLECTIVE LEVEL OF OF HUMAN CONSCIOUSNESS AND LOVE WILL BLOSSOM ON THE PLANET AGAIN WHICH IS LOST NOW DUE TO DUALITY.

Note: This is just a vague thought of the Author which can evolve as Currency Note or Certificate of Abundance traded on Exchanges just like Carbon Credit Certificates. Lets be Futuristic. Author laughs! but You Never Know as Source Knows it ALL.

CHAPTER SEVENTEEN

UNIVERSE HAS GOT YOUR BACK Everything is Going to be OKAY :)

This is the part where I tell you that you are safe, protected, cherished, and that the Universe has your back.

Don't believe me?

Well, if I can't convince you, just think about all the times your guides gave you good advice, in the form of a sign or number or message or synchronicity at just the right time. Everyone has a story, something they can't explain with 3D concepts.

The truth is, whether you heed their messages or not, you'll probably be okay, but wouldn't you rather be incredible? Awesome? Amazing?

Your guides want you to have everything you've ever dreamed of having. The Universe wants you to have these things, and more.

The Universe wants you to live the life you deserve. A life of joy, bliss, abundance, family, connection, peace, harmony, and a deep sense of purpose.

So, start paying attention to synchronicities, heed the signs, no matter how silly they seem.

Don't be afraid to make big changes in your life, and take that leap of faith, before the Universe picks you up and throws you off the cliff to get your attention.

You've got this :)

NEVER QUIT & KEEP ASKING FOR SIGNS

* THE UNIVERSE ALWAYS HAS YOUR BACK *

I WOULD ALWAYS SAY KEEP LISTENING TO SONG "WORK BITCH " BY BRITNEY SPEARS, AN EVER INSPIRING SONG TO RISE LIKE A PHOENIX FROM ASHES & "ROAR" BY KATE PERRY TO UPLIFT ONESELF FROM THE BIGGEST PITFALLS IN LIFE AND ROAR LIKE A LION AFTER FALLING AS YOU HAVE NO CHOICE, UNIVERSE WILL NOT LEAVE YOU TILL YOU GET YOUR DESIRED GOALS & MANISFESTATION.

* ALWAYS REMEMBER ABUNDANCE IS OUR BIRTH RIGHT*

Collective Abundance For Humanity & Lets Progress As Human Race

LETS ALL JOIN HANDS TO BRING COLLECTIVE ABUNDANCE FOR MOTHER GAIA & ENTIRE HUMAN FORCE ASCEND FROM DUALITY.

WE ALL KNOW DEEP INSIDE OUR HEARTS & IN OUR CONSCIOUSNESS THAT WE ALL JUST WANT TO PROVE OURSELVES AND SEPARATE OURSELVES FROM ONE ANOTHER TO FEED OUR EGO WHICH IS JUST AN ILLUSION AND OUR HEART BEATS FOR LOVE. LETS INSTRUCT OUR MIND TO LISTEN TO OUR HEART RATHER THAN CLOSING OUR HEART BY LISTENING TO OUR MIND WHICH IS A DEVIL AND ALWAYS WANTS US TO DO THE OPPOSITE AND ENTIRE HUMANITY TOGETHER UNHAPPY BUT EGOISTIC TO ACCEPT IT. WE SEEM TO BE IN A RACE TO DEFEAT ONE ANOTHER OR PROVE OURSELVES FOR ACCEPTANCE WHICH IS WHY WE ARE COLLECTIVELY HEADING TOWARDS MASS DESTRUCTION AND WAR FOR SUFFERING AND FUTURE CAN BE WORSE AS WE ALREADY SAW COVID-19, RUSSIA-UKRAINE WAR, SRILANKA & NEPAL MISERY etc.

ITS A WAKE UP CALL FOR EVERYONE TO USE OUR EDUCATION AND INTELLECT WHICH GOD HAS GIVEN TO US FOR RIGHTEOUSNESS, AND LIFTING EACH OTHER UP FROM PITFALLS AND LISTEN TO OUR HEART INTUITIVELY WHICH IS THE ESSENCE OF LOVING OURSELVES AND SHARING LOVE WITH ENTIRE HUMANITY AS WE ALL ARE ONE AND NOT SEPARATE.

IF ALMIGHTY HAS NEVER DISTINGUISHED US OR CREATED NATION, LANGUAGE, RELIGION, RACE ETC, WE ARE JUST A TINY DOT TO DO IT. SO LETS BEAT OUR HEARTS FOR LOVING ONE ANOTHER AND UPLIFT OURSLEVES FOR BETTER CAUSES AND USE TECHNOLOGY FOR PROGRESSION OF HUMAN RACE & NOT FOR MAKING NUCLEAR WEAPONS, ARMS & AMMUNITION TO TERROR AND FRIGHTEN ONE ANOTHER AS THIS WILL NEVER BRING ABUNDNANCE IN OUR LIFES AND WE WILL ALWAYS OPERATE AT LOW LEVEL OF CONSCIOUSNESS AND CONTINUE TO ATTRACT MISERY RATHER THAN PURE FORM OF LOVE, HAPPINESS, PEACE, FULFILLMENT. DO CHARITY AS THE LAW OF UNIVERSE IS GOVERNED ON THE PRINCIPLE OF

"MORE WE GIVE MORE WE SHALL RECEIVE

&

AGAIN MORE WE RECEIVE MORE WE GIVE"

PLEASE REFER TO LEVEL OF CONSCIOUSNESS BELOW FOR EACH EMOTION WE EXHIBIT IN OUR DAILY LIVES AS WE SHOULD COME TO A LEVEL OF ABOVE 600 TO MANIFEST ABUNDANCE. SO EACH ONE OF US MUST COME TO LEVEL OF CONSCIOUNESS ABOVE 600 IN ORDER TO BRING COLLECTIVE ABUNDANCE AS EVEN SOME INDIVIDUALS MIGHT BE HAVING BUT IF WE DONT GROW HIGHER AS COLLECTIVE CONSCIOUSNESS WE WILL BE HEADING FOR A DRAUGHT PHASE OR EXTINCTION AS COVID-19, RUSSIA-UKRAINE WAR, SRILANKA & NEPAL TRAGEDY, AND SOONER TRAGEDIES TO ALL OUR COUNTRIES. LETS EDUCATE AND SHARE THIS WITH EVERYONE TO HEAL THE ENTIRE PLANET BY RAISING OUR CONSCIOUNESS BY FOLLOWING

CERTAIN TOOLS I HAVE MENTIONED IN THE BOOK & BE AWARE OF EMOTIONS WE GENERATE AND OUR INNER VOICE AND NEGATIVE SELF TALK AS

"I HAVE PERSONALLY EXPERIENCED THAT ALL OUR THOUGHTS, EMOTIONS AND FEELING

VIBRATE AT A FREQUENCY AND THEY ARE RECORDED IN THE UNIVERSE. "

SO WHAT WE EMOTE AND THINK IS WHAT WE ATTRACT.

UNIVERSE WORKS ON THIS PRINCIPLES. HENCE WE ALL SEE COVID-19 AS A MAJOR SETBACK WE ALL AS HUMAN BEINGS ATTRACTED SINCE WE ARE COLLECTIVELY OPERATING AT VIBRATION OF 150 TO 200 WHICH WILL ATTRACT ONLY DESTRUCTION FOR US AND WE SHOULD STOP BLAMING EACH OTHER FOR THE CAUSE AS BLAMING IS THE LOWEST LEVEL OF CONSCIOUSNESS AND WE SHOULD FORGET THE PAST AND FORGIVE ONE ANOTHER AND TYPE A RESET BUTTON IN OUR LIFE.

LETS COLLECTIVELY OWN RESPONSIBILTY TOWARDS MOTHER GAIA AND NOW IT'S OUR TIME TO GIVE TO OUR MOTHER PLANET AS SHE HAS LOVED US LIKE HER BABIES AND GIVEN SELFLESSLY TO US: FOOD AND WEALTH, BUT WE HAVE SHOWN OUR BACK TOWARDS HER BY BEING SELFISH. NOW OUR MOTHER GAIA HAS REACHED A LEVEL WHERE SHE CANNOT GIVE ANY MORE & CANNOT BEAR THE PAIN ANYMORE HENCE WE ALL ARE COLLECTIVELY FACING ISSUES WORSE THAN COVID-19 OR WAR IN THE NEAR FUTURE AND NEVER KNOW WE HEAD FOR EXTINCTION.

I WILL EXPLAIN SERIOUSNESS OF MY CONCLUSION ABOVE IN MUCH DETAILS WITH THE

HELP OF A SIMPLE EXAMPLE BUT VERY CRUCIAL FOR US TO PAY ATTENTION TO

"JUST LIKE WE AS HUMAN BEINGS ARE CELLS IN THE BODY OF MOTHER GAIA EARTH, IF ONE CELL OF A HUMAN BODY DYSFUNCTIONS THE BODY WILL ATTRACT DISEASE AND IF MORE THAN 50 PERCENT DON'T FUNCTION WELL, OUR BODY CAN BECOME FATAL OR HEADING TOWARDS IT. IMAGINE US TO BE PART OF MOTHER GAIA EARTHS BODY WHERE ATLEAST 50 PERCENT ARE DYSFUNCTIONING AND ARE AT LOWEST LEVEL OF CONSCIOUSNESS WHICH I SAY AS DEAD CELLS NATUTRALLY OVERALL PLANET WILL COLLAPSE"

*Please find the table below for knowing the count and measuring ourselves as Levels of Consciousness and Emotions we operate at.

"

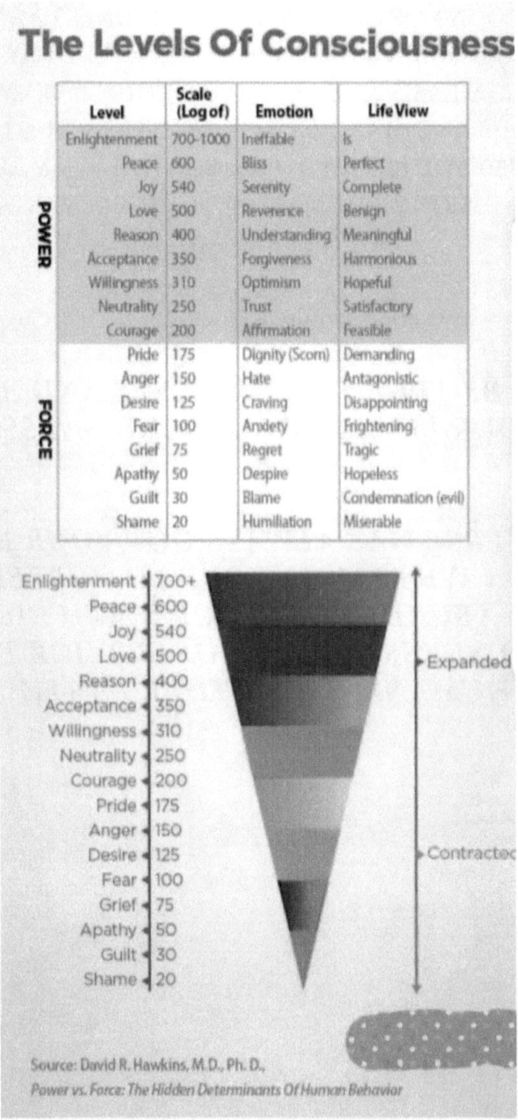

The Levels Of Consciousness

	Level	Scale (Log of)	Emotion	Life View
POWER	Enlightenment	700-1000	Ineffable	Is
	Peace	600	Bliss	Perfect
	Joy	540	Serenity	Complete
	Love	500	Reverence	Benign
	Reason	400	Understanding	Meaningful
	Acceptance	350	Forgiveness	Harmonious
	Willingness	310	Optimism	Hopeful
	Neutrality	250	Trust	Satisfactory
	Courage	200	Affirmation	Feasible
FORCE	Pride	175	Dignity (Scorn)	Demanding
	Anger	150	Hate	Antagonistic
	Desire	125	Craving	Disappointing
	Fear	100	Anxiety	Frightening
	Grief	75	Regret	Tragic
	Apathy	50	Despire	Hopeless
	Guilt	30	Blame	Condemnation (evil)
	Shame	20	Humiliation	Miserable

Source: David R. Hawkins, M.D., Ph. D.,
Power vs. Force: The Hidden Determinants Of Human Behavior

THE TABLE ABOVE IS FOR SELF EVALUATION OF
COUNT OF OUR OWN CONSCIOUNESS AND
EMOTIONS WE OPERATE AT, ON EVERY DAY OR
HOURLY BASIS AND LETS CONSCIOUSLY BE AWARE
OF THIS AND MAKE AN EFFORT TO REACH A LEVEL
OF 550 AND SLOWY TO 650 SO THAT WE MAKE A
PROGRESSION AS HUMAN RACE AND BE AT STATE OF
LOVE, PEACE AND JOY

We don't require a Doctor to measure us,

***LETS BE TRUE TO OURSELVES AND RAISE
OUR LEVEL OF CONSCIOUSNESS,***

***UNIVERSE HAS ALWAYS GOT YOUR BACK
WHEN WE REMAIN TRUE TO OURSELVES
AND ABUNDANCE IS OUR BIRTH RIGHT,
SO NEVER QUIT, BE OF SERVICE TO
HUMANITY & MOTHER EARTH"***